Sounds All Around

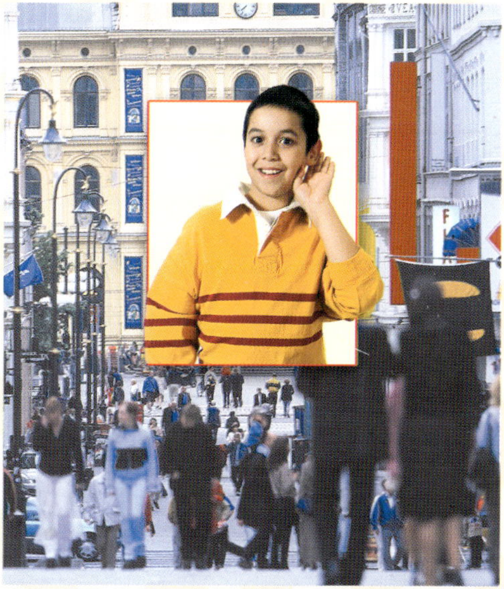

Joanne Wachter

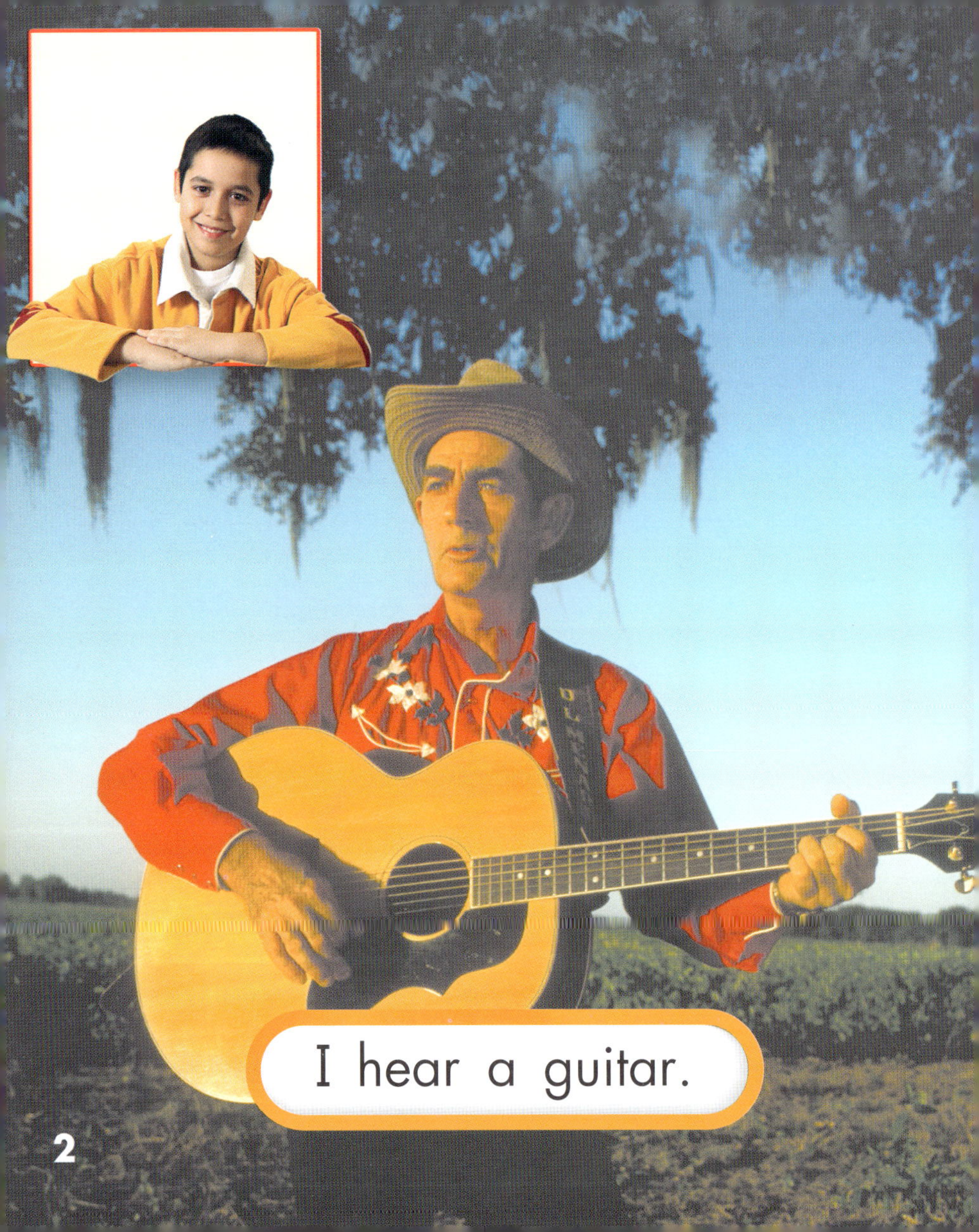

I hear a guitar.

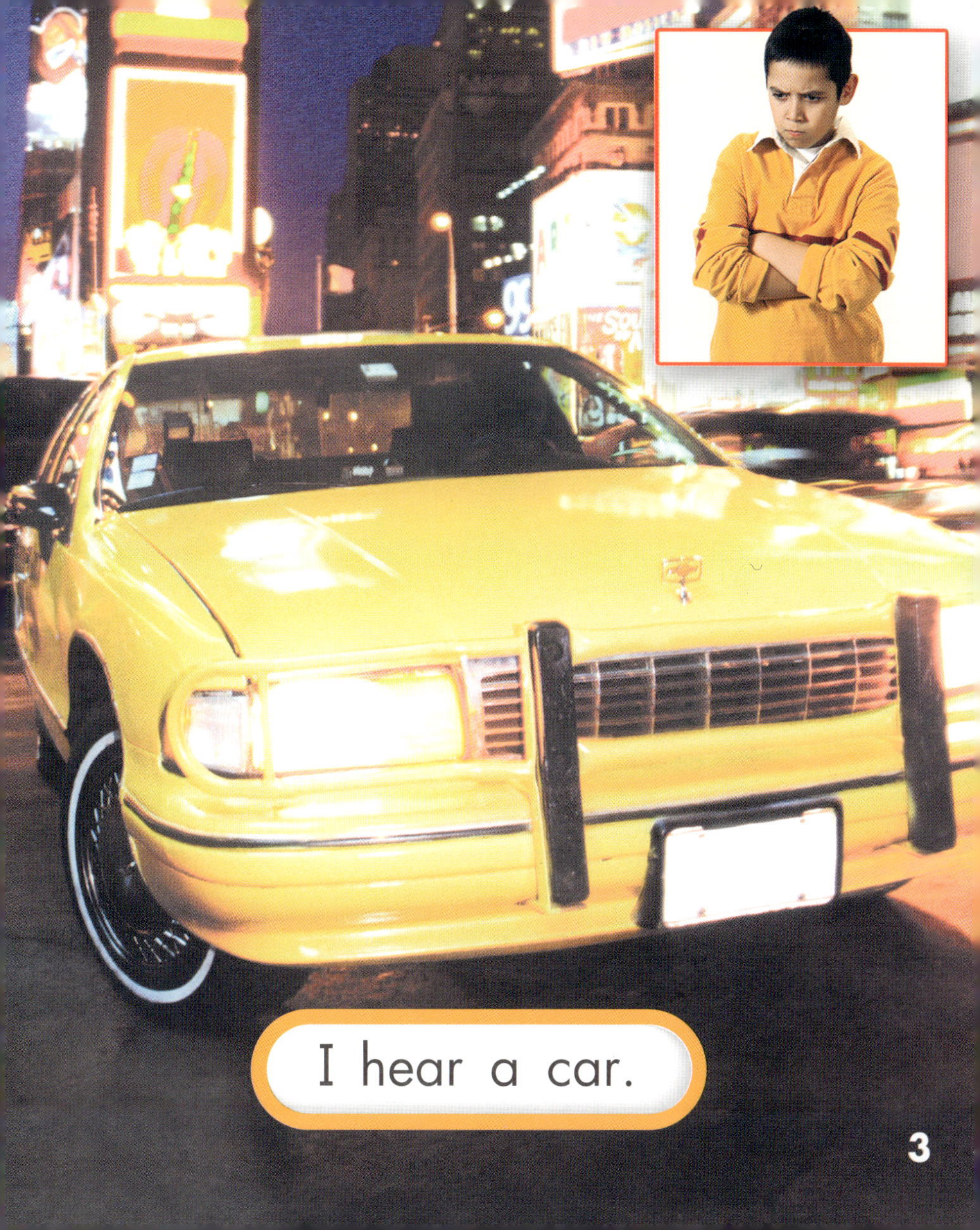

I hear a car.

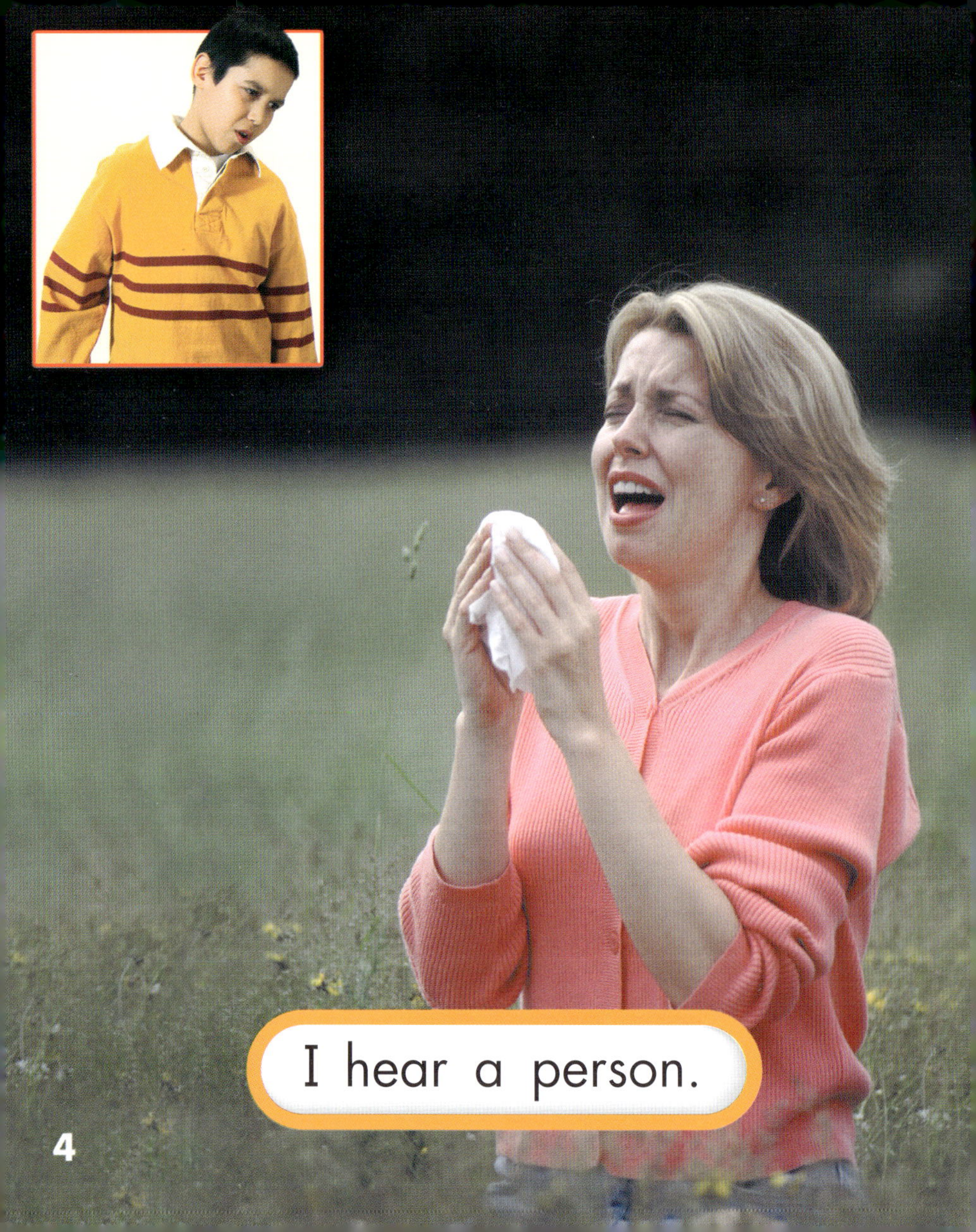

I hear a person.

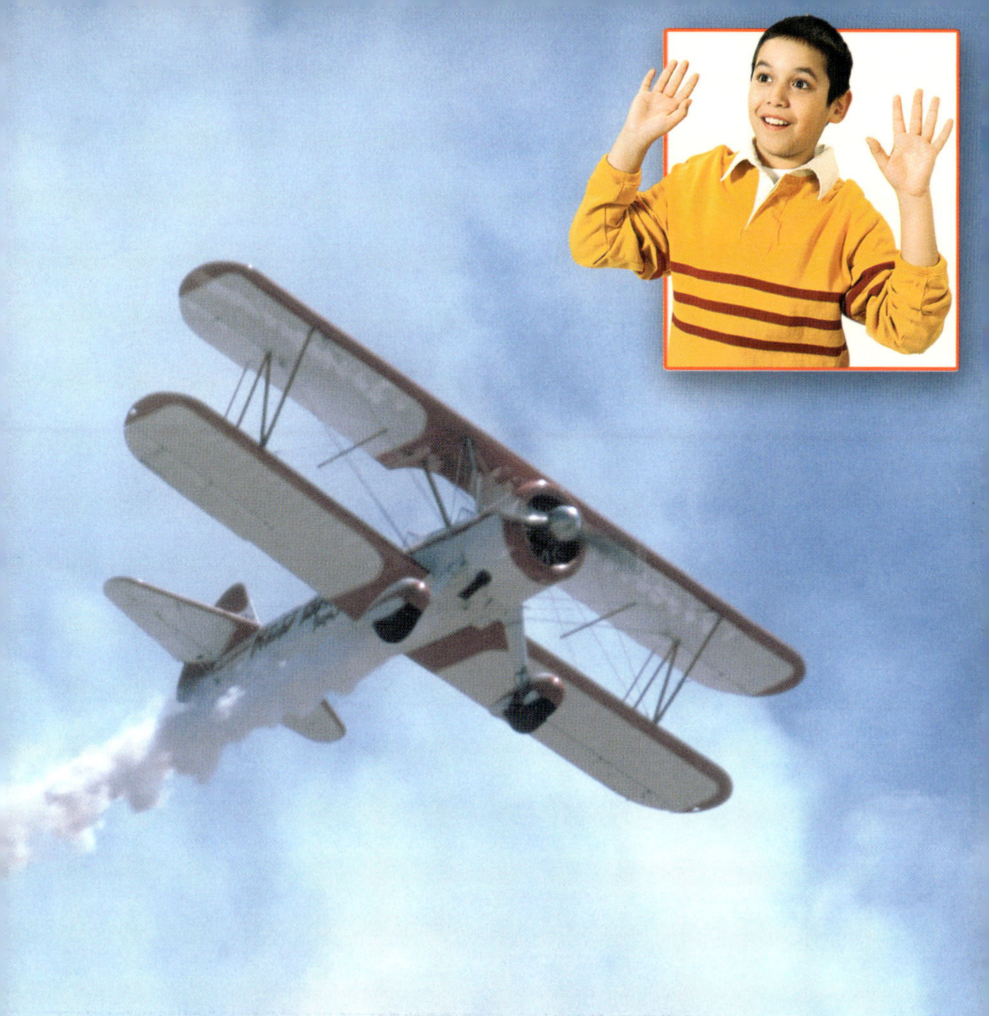

I hear a plane.

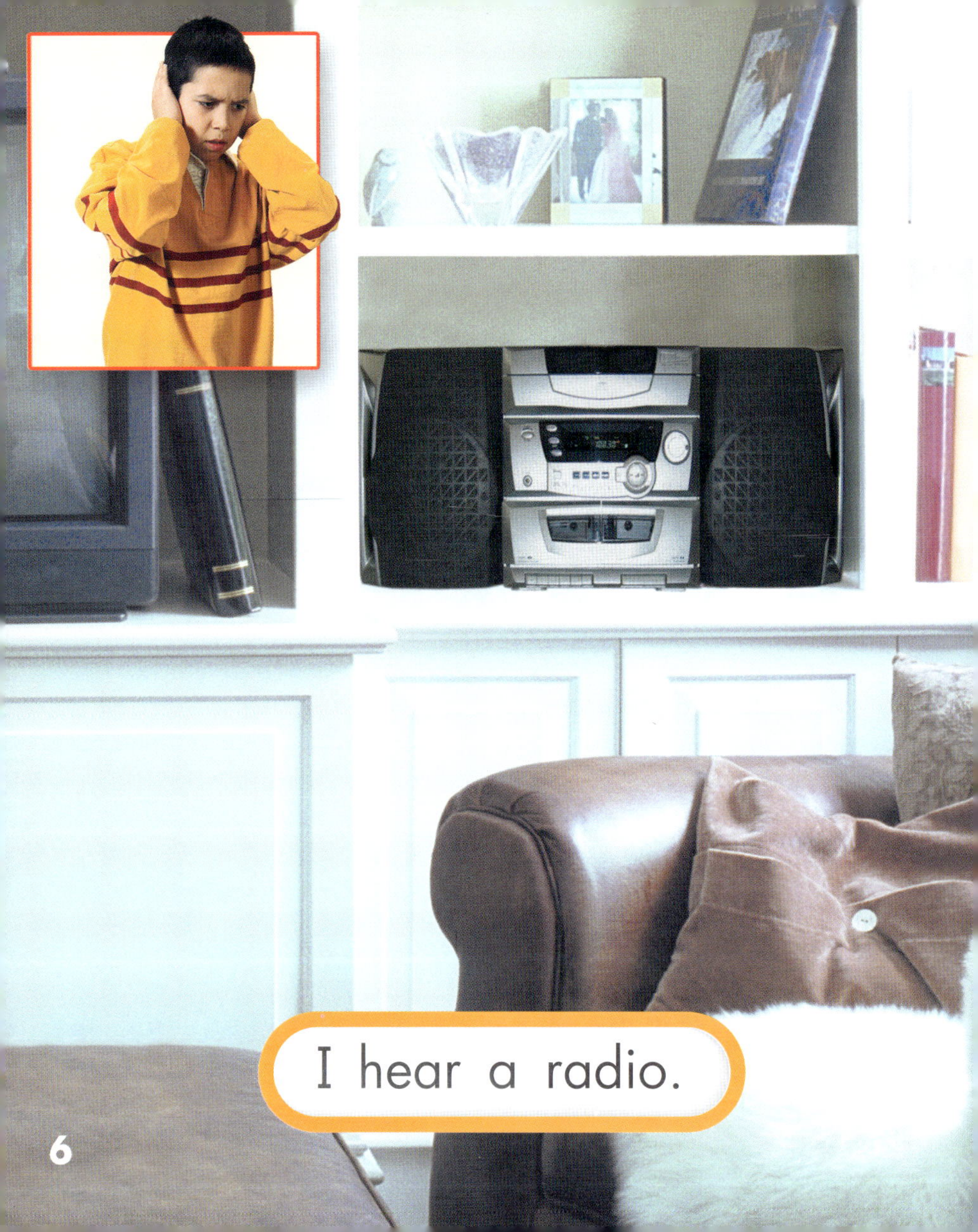

I hear a radio.

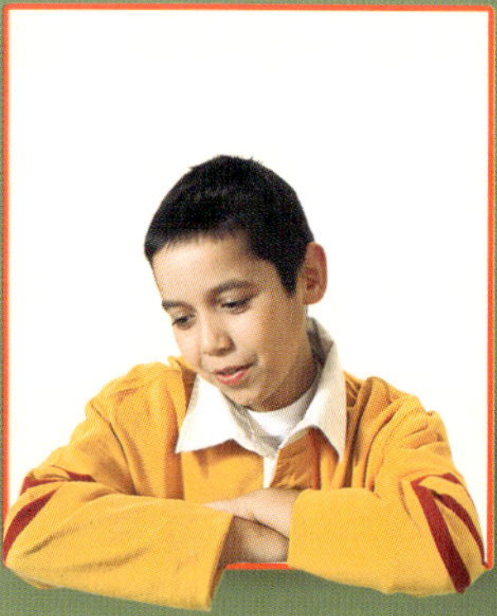

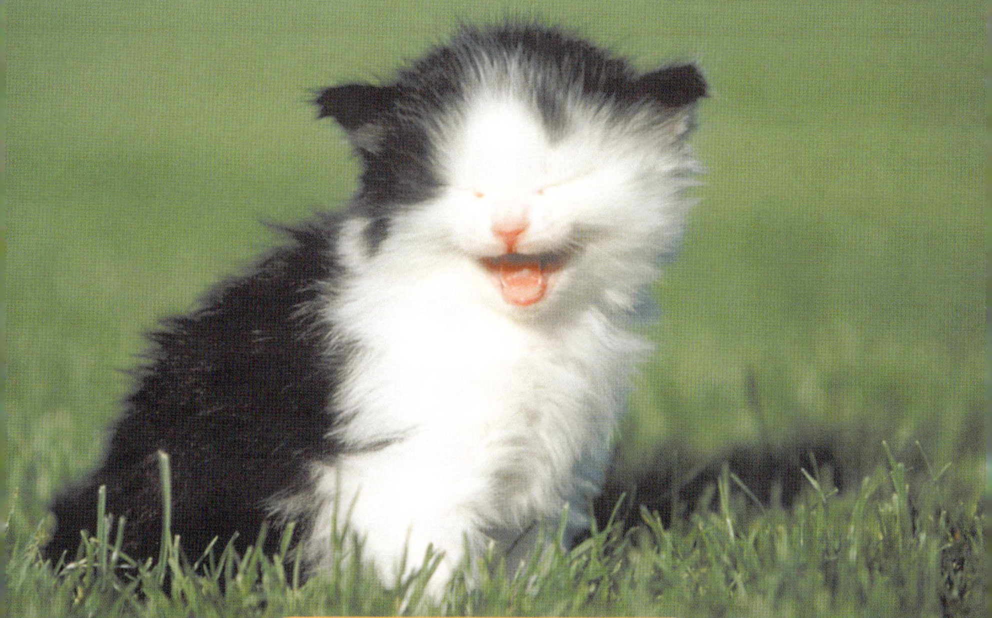

I hear a kitten.

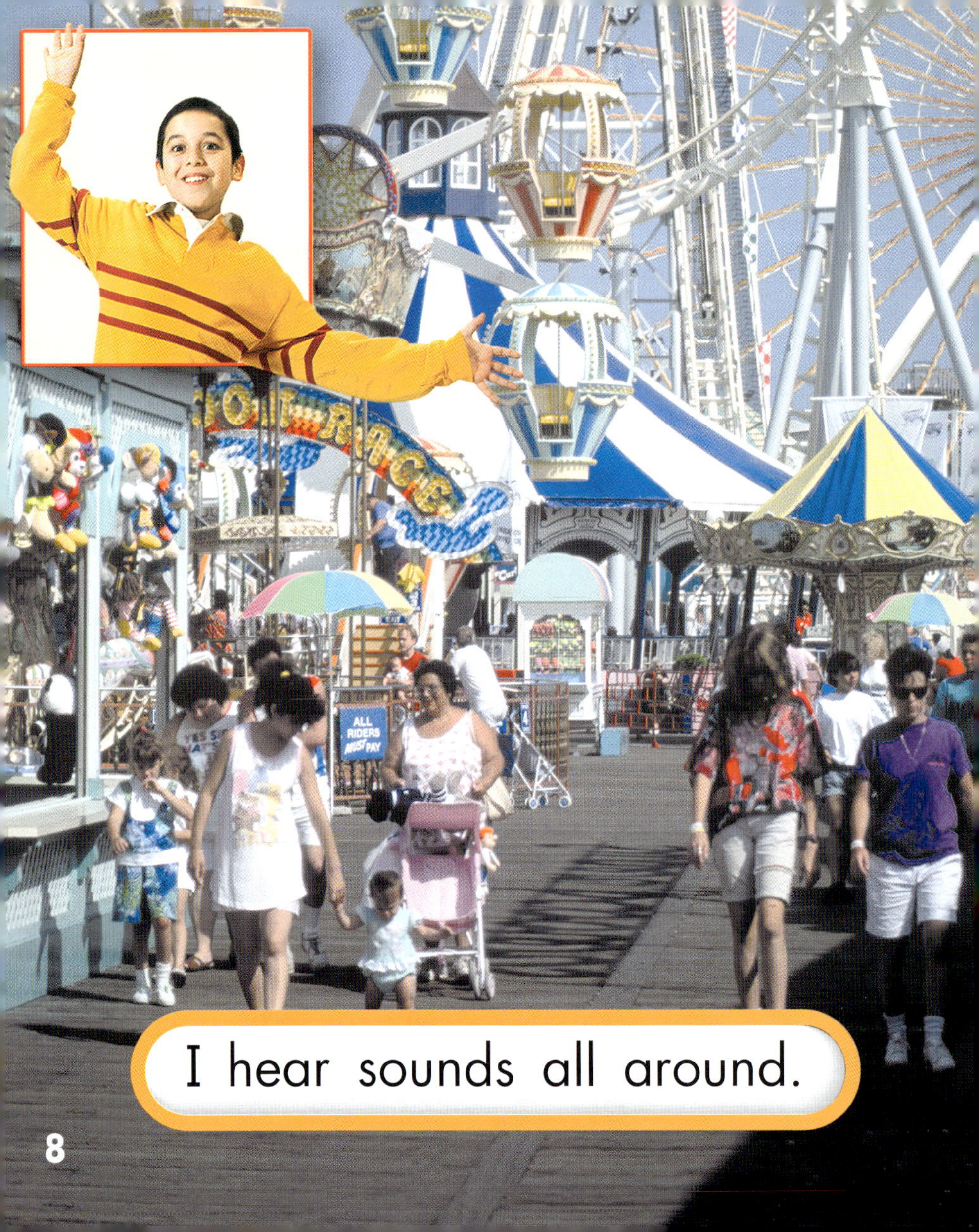

I hear sounds all around.